# Leadership

Key Competencies For Inspiring And Exerting Influence On Individuals In Your Surroundings Optimize Your Capacity For Leadership

*(Elevate Your Leadership Voyage One Minute At A Time)*

**Tomas Pennington**

# TABLE OF CONTENT

# Precisely, What Is A Leader?

The term "leader" evokes an assortment of mental images. For instance, consider a political leader ardently dedicated to a cause of profound personal significance.

● An intrepid explorer embarking on an expedition into uncharted territories. ● An executive is devising tactics to accomplish the objectives of the organization.

Diverse perspectives exist regarding who ought to assume leadership roles. As opposed to the conventional "top-down" approach, Michael Useem, a professor of management, argues that bottom-up leadership is more effective. Furthermore, leadership in today's complex, globalized workplaces can originate from various sources. Certain organizations may find that the executives occupying supervisory positions possess the most influence. Managers are, after all, the individuals who interact with teams the most.

Leadership is no longer regarded as an individual pursuit. As an increasing number of organizations grow too large and complex for a single leader to oversee individually, distributed leadership, which originates in the education field, is gaining popularity.

## Why Is Leadership Precisely So Vital?

In every industry, effective leadership is essential. Well-led organizations are generally characterized by increased productivity, competitiveness, and adaptability to change. A greater comprehension of their objectives and rationales fosters greater employee engagement and motivation. A propensity for producing leaders increases the long-term profitability of an organization.

For the achievement of your organization, you require strong leaders. The work environment can be enhanced by concentrating on developing and improving leadership skills. Organizations necessitate a leadership development strategy to consistently have capable and confident personnel in positions of power. An effective leadership development strategy can profoundly influence the entire organization, surpassing the mere presence of a competent leader.

Leadership Development's Positive Aspects

Future leaders can be instructed— Assembling individuals who exhibit exceptional potential for leadership positions, a company that allocates resources towards workforce development invests in the future. By enhancing the skill sets of existing personnel via leadership development, they transform into the most promising individuals capable of effecting positive, long-lasting change.

Increases Productivity By utilizing a leadership development program, leaders enhance their capacity to recognize challenges, generate novel concepts, and effectively manage obstacles; these attributes collectively contribute to an overall increase in workforce productivity.

Improved Retention of Top Talent—Employee loyalty and retention can be enhanced when personnel acquire new competencies and assume additional responsibilities. A prevalent factor contributing to employee attrition is inadequate leadership. An organization's workforce will exhibit increased tenure in response to a leader with adequate leadership development training designed for current leaders.

Facilitates Organisational Changes—Seconds are prevalent in an industry, and employees are more adept at adjusting to changes in the workplace, including reorganizations and the entry of new competitors, when an exceptional leader is in position.

Effective leadership development can significantly affect the profitability of an organization. Enhanced employee retention can yield favorable consequences for organizations, including heightened employee engagement and Productivity and a constructive influence on the company's culture.

Leadership development can be administered and instructed in numerous ways. Commence your journey towards developing your leadership abilities with the assistance of an executive coach so that you can have a greater influence and effect significant changes for your team.

Attributes of a Proficient Leader

Acquiring a compelling principle and assembling a team to implement that principle consistently constitute the fundamental steps in establishing a prosperous organization. Although discovering a novel and unique tip may seem unusual, the ability to execute this concept successfully divides the daydreamers from the business professionals. You become aware of your progress, regardless of how mature you may become, the moment you complete that exhilarating initial hire; you have, in reality, embarked on the initial phase of becoming an exceptionally valuable pioneer. When finances are limited, levels of anxiety increase, and expectations of immediate results do not materialize as one might anticipate. However, it is simple and quick to enable these emotional states to affect you and your staff. Take a deep inhale, bring yourself into a state of calmness, and give yourself feedback regarding the innovator you are at present and aspire to become. Detailed below are several essential qualities that every effective leader should possess, along with strategies for coping with anxiety.

True sincerity

Regardless of the straightforward aircraft you choose to operate your business, it is crucial to elevate the club to an even greater degree when you manage a staff of individuals. Your organization and its personnel reflect your character; therefore, if you prioritize ethical and transparent conduct, your staff will undoubtedly follow suit.

As we do at One Vest, the community funding platform for local businesses and entrepreneurs I co-founded, you and your label should compile a list of qualities and fundamental concepts that you and your organization embody. Please display this document in your workplace. Advocate for adopting a healthy interoffice routine in daily life and encourage your team to assess to these extents. By emphasizing these standards and demonstrating them personally, you are potentially influencing the office environment to become a friendly and supportive workplace.

The Ability to Delegate

Improving your brand's attitude is crucial for establishing a successful and operational business. However, if you fail to establish credibility for your team with that attitude, you will fail to advance to the subsequent phase. It is critical to remember that withdrawing your team from consideration and your suggestion indicates strength, not weakness.

Understanding the strengths of one's team and capitalizing on each of them is the key to effective delegation. Learn precisely what each employee takes pleasure in performing.

The exchange of communications

Indeed, the ability to precisely and succinctly articulate precisely what you desire is crucial. You will not be collectively working towards the same objective if you cannot link your vision with your staff.

Establishing a successful office and educating new employees depend on a balanced and well-balanced set of interactions. Whether that is achieved through implementing a visible entrance plan in your workplace or by establishing a daily suggestion line with your staff, having a personal assessment area for interoffice concerns is crucial. Your employees will develop a sense of trust in you and become considerably less resistant to the prospect of exerting greater effort.

Amusing bone

Indeed, a correlation exists between mindset and efficacy; therefore, as the staff trendsetter, it is incumbent upon you to inspire an exceptional force. By consistently striving to find humor in difficult situations, your workplace will undoubtedly evolve into a joyful and healthy environment where employees look forward to working rather than fearing it. These time-outs that are made available through the duty useful prevent attitudes from becoming even more negative and productivity levels from rising significantly.

Our professional setting is dog-friendly, and our team truly believes that these brief, lighthearted moments keep our tasks fresh and functional. An exemplary practice that our organization endeavors to uphold and imparts to the group is the preparation of a remarkable secret regarding all newly hired personnel on their initial day.

## The Guaranteed

Fire extinguishing and ensuring the team's well-being are essential responsibilities of a leader. As the trailblazer, by maintaining composure and concentration, you will undoubtedly assist the team in avoiding the same. Remember that your team will undoubtedly interpret your signals; therefore, if you demonstrate a certain degree of composure under pressure, they will surely perceive that as such.

## Required Action

If you expect your team to exert effort and deliver high-quality online content, you are essentially arranging for yourself to be required to set an exemplary example. Demonstrating your dedication to both the organization and your role will earn your colleagues' admiration and inspire the same level of diligence in one of your personnel. Once you have earned the respect of your staff, they are considerably more inclined to provide the highest possible volume of fee work.

# The Determination Of Purpose

Napoleon Hill wrote the following in Think and Grow Rich:

Indeed, "thoughts are things," and formidable ones, when combined with determination, persistence, and an intense longing to transform them into material wealth or other tangible possessions.

To clarify this proverb, he is essentially attempting to teach us that when we consider something—for instance, "By tomorrow, I hope to have completed this book"—that is not what it means.

Should I express such a sentiment with genuine intention and a sincere desire to carry it out, it could be due to a compelling reason that compels me to surpass my customary capabilities. Typing will not tire my limbs; even if it does, I will continue. Constantly contemplating my objective, I exert every effort possible to attain it. Maintain a supply of coffee, break for ten minutes each hour to stretch and re-energize, and set word count deadlines for myself at the hour. These constraints determined the word count per hour I needed to produce to meet my objective.

Ultimately, I'm willing to wager that I would have come quite near to reaching my objective, even if I fall short. The term "definiteness of purpose" refers to this. It is awakening with a specific objective and taking actionable measures toward its realization. It is said that aiming for the moon could result in encountering the constellations. However, without some knowledge of space travel, including the cost and prerequisites for boarding a vessel, physical health requirements, and so forth, it is impossible to simply aim for it.

In other words, success and attaining one's objectives do not hinge on hoping and having faith that one's desires are realized. It entails designating a specific objective with as much specificity as possible and acquiring the necessary knowledge and/or experience to materialize that aspiration. That is the clarity of your intent. A definite meaning is characterized by an objective that is precise, particular, quantifiable, mutually agreed upon, practical, and time-bound.

Create a distinct and precise success objective before you begin. For instance, one might aspire to acquire an ideal home. Ensure the objective is quantifiable and measurable. This enables you to specify the number of rooms, the size of the compound, the materials to be used in the home's construction, and so forth. Ascertain that the objective is both plausible and attainable.

Once, Canadian rapper Aubrey Drake Graham recounted to GQ magazine how he spotted his dream home when he was seventeen years old. He utilized a photograph of that residence for five years as his screen saver. It was by his twenty-fourth birthday that he had moved into that residence. Your assessment of its plausibility and feasibility is, therefore, what matters. You will determine whether you have a reasonable chance of success in this manner.

Start modestly to exercise your thinking muscles initially. Commence with objectives you possess a moderately high likelihood of achieving within a brief period. Develop your abilities as you establish more challenging objectives.

Second Chapter

Acknowledging your troops

T

Particularly in instances of commendation, one significantly influences how others interpret a leader's intended message. A leader should exercise extreme caution to avoid offending individuals, even when bestowing praise or recognition. Kindness and affection must be demonstrated during this portion of the conversation; otherwise, the associate may perceive you as speaking at them instead of with them.

It is evident that the reception of a message is determined by individual perception, irrespective of the sender's intentions; tone serves as the determining factor. There have been occasions when I extended congratulations to others but was so physically and mentally exhausted that the tone of my message appeared contrived and indifferent.

Proper manifestation can only occur when leaders devote their entire being to the task. The Holy Spirit can manifest within a given area after establishing an intention and adhering to divine guidance.

This facilitates the application of anointing and enables you to serve as a guiding light for an individual needing reassurance. Your responsibility as a leader is to demonstrate to your subordinates that trivial matters should not bother them. Possessing this mindset is one thing; however, you must exercise caution when explaining it to another individual.

Prior experiences have demonstrated that an aspect that seems inconsequential to one person may appear turbulent to another when viewed from a different perspective. While a leader needs to respect an associate's feelings, establishing boundaries is crucial to prevent this individual from dwelling on negative emotions that past experiences may trigger.

Minor details, such as disclosing personal challenges that an individual successfully surmounted, can potentially cause embarrassment for that person even though their perseverance and determination are being commended.

Concerning the Matter of Trust

The foundational study that underpins the work of my colleagues and me and this book was of the Human Resources Laboratory of South Africa during the early 1980s. The research was conducted as part of an initiative to investigate employee discontent. My book 'Beyond Management' provides a more comprehensive account of this research. Essentially, that study aimed to investigate employees' confidence in mine management. It was predicated on the notion that employees would be content if they had faith in their managers; conversely, discontentment would result if they had faith in their managers.

The research findings exhibited noteworthy discrepancies among the mines, the patterns of which have taken us by surprise. Notwithstanding the severe labor conditions that were in place at the time (apartheid was in full swing in the conservative South African mining industry), they hypothesized that there was not necessarily an absolute Marxist chasm between employers and employees that rendered it impossible for workers to have faith in management.

The unexpected outcomes incited inquiries: "What factors could account for the divergent degrees of trust?" Why did workers at one mine have faith in their supervisors while those at another mine had no faith in them?"

We combed through the relevant literature and conducted interviews with various industry managers in search of plausible explanations to validate against the data we had collected. Although the initial list of potential explanations was quite extensive, we ultimately achieved success in condensing it to the subsequent factors:

Physical circumstances

"If employees are housed in substandard housing or are required to work in hazardous and difficult conditions, they will not trust management," was the hypothesis. However, our research findings indicated that trust in management was significantly lower at a large modern mine, despite the favorable conditions, compared to every other mine examined in the study (including those with genuinely Dickensian environmental conditions).

Labour combination

"For historical, cultural, or other reasons, different groups of men have different predispositions toward the industry," was the hypothesis. This hypothesis pertained to intricate historical and cultural generalizations concerning laborers who spoke Shangaan, Sotho, or Xhosa. However, the results indicated that while Shangaans as a collective tended to have a higher level of trust in their managers, as predicted by the hypothesis, this trend was so mine-specific that it could not fundamentally explain the problem of trust in management.

Rates of compensation

The hypothesis posited in this instance was that "individuals will lack trust in management if they are not adequately compensated." However, the outcome demonstrated that whether you pay your employees the industry minimum or maximum wage is inconsequential and will not influence the degree to which they place their trust in you.

Politics-related factors

The proposition was as follows: "The ongoing political disputes at the local and national levels directly impact trust in management." This hypothesis was predicated on the notion that black employees would continue to channel their political grievances into the workplace in the absence of a political resolution. Nevertheless, the findings revealed significant variations in levels of trust across divisions of a single mine, even though all employees had equal access to local communities and, by extension, the broader political discourse. This suggests that the claim was not entirely accurate. A mine near one of the most politically charged municipalities in the nation exhibited a notable degree of employee confidence in the management.

## THE CONTROVERSIAL MODEL

This pertains to a cohort comprising individuals led by a conventional supervisor yet also bearing a portion of the accountability and power. Generally, the revealed amount depends on the subject matter being discussed. A particular individual is in command but may occasionally delegate leadership responsibilities to other team members.

## MODEL OF THE TEAM SPIRIT

This group of employees appears to be content with their position under the same supervisor, and everything appears to proceed smoothly. While some individuals exhibit a sense of camaraderie, they fail to function as a cohesive unit due to a unilateral decision-maker who does not delegate authority or accountability.

THE MODEL OF CUTTING-EDGE

This group consists of individuals who manage themselves. No single member of the group has the authority to decide on every aspect of the events that affect the group. This group is called a self-directed work team because each individual possesses authority and accountability for every decision that must be reached.

The model of task forces

This group assembles for a designated period to complete a particular mission or project. Historically referred to as a task force or committee, this organization may consist of quality circles (as utilized in TQM initiatives).

The Cyber Group

Within this particular team paradigm, members have minimal or no face-to-face interactions. These are referred to as virtual or cyber teams.

Differentiating these teams is that they must collaborate to achieve objectives; however, they may only convene briefly at the outset of the project and then communicate via telephone and email afterward. Additionally, they are compatible with all four models shown above.

Knowledge type one can assist in determining the most effective approach to work planning and establishingestablishtations for desired outcomes.

The definition of a team

shared responsibility, and conscious leadership to accomplish predetermined objectives in an advantageous manner to all parties involved.

If you disjustify justified, do you justify each term and phrase in dissection?

As a leader, what are the most productive approaches to conflict resolution and managing challenging circumstances?

Difficult circumstances and conflict are unavoidable in any group or organization; therefore, effective leaders must be able to manage them constructively and optimistically. The subsequent strategies are applicable for leaders to implement when confronted with conflict and daunting circumstances:

Leaders should actively and empathetically listen to all parties involved in a challenging situation or conflict. This entails affording every individual the chance to articulate their viewpoint without interruptions while demonstrating authentic curiosity in comprehending their stance.

**Remain professional and composed:** Leaders should maintain professionalism and composure despite intense situations or strong emotions. This maintains order and fosters a respectful and secure atmosphere for all participants.

Leaders should concentrate on each party's fundamental requirements and interests instead of becoming mired in their positions or opinions. This facilitates the identification of areas of agreement and the development of solutions that benefit all parties involved.

Leaders should search for areas of agreement or shared objectives and then work to find a solution that is advantageous to both parties.

Leaders ought to employ effective communication strategies characterized by clarity, respect, and a lack of blame, accusations, or criticism. Instead, they should concentrate on resolving the issue at hand.

Leaders should seek input and feedback from all parties involved and negotiate in good faith to reach a solution on which all parties can reach an agreement.

**Following up:** Leaders should conduct post-resolution follow-ups with all parties involved in a challenging situation or conflict to ascertain the resolution's effectiveness and identify any additional concerns that may require attention.

In essence, effective leadership entails active listening, maintaining composure and professionalism, directing attention towards shared interests rather than rigid stances, striving for consensus, employing efficient communication methods, engaging in collaborative and negotiating processes, and conducting follow-up assessments to validate the efficacy of proposed resolutions. By applying these strategies, leaders can construct more resilient and robust teams by transforming adversity and conflict into opportunities for growth and development.

What strategies can leaders employ to foster a constructive and encouraging corporate environment that facilitates the advancement and progress of its members?

Establishing a constructive and positive corporate environment is critical for fostering the progress and advancement of personnel and is fundamental to the achievement of any institution. Leaders may implement the following techniques to foster a constructive and positive organizational culture:

Leadership should define and communicate the organization's fundamental values, reflecting its mission, vision, and objectives. All facets of the organization, including policies, procedures, and decision-making processes, ought to reflect these values.

**Encourage open communication:** Leaders should foster an environment where team members feel secure sharing their ideas and opinions by encouraging open communication. This can be accomplished using routine team meetings, feedback sessions, and additional modes of communication.

Leaders should provide opportunities for growth and development, including mentoring, employment rotations, and training programs, so that team members may expand their knowledge and abilities. This contributes to the development and evolution of team members and the retention of top talent.

**Acknowledge and reward accomplishments:** Leaders are responsible for acknowledging and rewarding team members' contributions and accomplishments. This can be accomplished via formal or informal sincere expressions of gratitude via thank-you notes or verbal commendation.

**Foster a positive work environment:** Leaders should promote collaboration, cooperation, and respect while fostering a positive work environment. This can be accomplished by fostering a supportive workplace environment, encouraging work-life balance, and providing opportunities for social interaction.

Lastly, leaders should demonstrate the values and conduct they anticipate from their team members through their actions. This requires demonstrating accountability, integrity, and a willingness to collaborate with team members.

In conclusion, establishing a constructive and favorable organizational climate necessitates establishing and disseminating fundamental principles, promoting candid dialogue, providing avenues for progress and advancement, acknowledging and incentivizing accomplishments, cultivating a positive workplace atmosphere, and displaying exemplary conduct. Leaders can establish a culture that fosters the progress and development of their team members, increases efficiency, and propels the organization's triumph by putting these strategies into practice.

The Importance of Equity at Work

Baronowski-Schneider, Patricia

Typically, when I consider equity, the stock market comes to mind. However, equity encompasses considerably more than mere investments. Both business and life contain equity, which are both current popular topics. Everyone is speaking of the concepts of equity and equality in the business world and the news.

Equality and equity are not synonymous. Equal treatment for all is the definition of equality, notwithstanding individual differences. Equality entails providing all individuals with the resources necessary for success.

Equity, as opposed to equality, pertains to fairness and justice. In contrast to equality, which entails that all individuals receive the same benefit, equity recognizes that not everyone begins in the same place and that disparities must be identified and rectified.

Equality and equity are necessary to guarantee justice and fairness and enable each individual in society to realize their complete capabilities. Equity seeks to provide individuals with the means to capitalize on those opportunities, whereas equality guarantees that all individuals are afforded equivalent opportunities.

Establishing equality in the workplace entails affording each employee, by their unique requirements, equitable and equal opportunities.

Equal opportunity is a wonderful thing to have in the workplace. The effort required to achieve a more equitable workplace is worth the endeavor.

Expanding the population of employees who can advance within an organization and contribute to a future with more diverse leaders is what equality in the workplace entails.

Fostering an equitable work environment requires an investment in personnel, and equality can additionally increase employee engagement and retention. Employees are inclined to be more loyal to organizations that demonstrate concern for their well-being. According to research, more than 150 percent of employees who experience a sense of belonging at work are 34% more likely to recommend their employer and are more inclined to remain.

There is a reason why an increasing number of businesses are dedicating resources to enhancing their equity. According to a 2021 CNBC survey, increasing employees desire employment with organizations that value equity.

A further 2019 report finds that organizations led by a greater proportion of women are 25% more likely to achieve above-average profitability than organizations ranked in the bottom quartile. A company's reputation could be enhanced in light of the increasing demand for equality by investing in employee diversity and competence, thereby contributing to a more proficient and proficient workforce.

Leaders establish equity in the workforce by ensuring that each employee has the necessary access, opportunities, and promotion to succeed. This empowers employees to contribute diverse perspectives, expertise, and ideas that enhance the company's ability to cater to its consumers and grow. What is the significance of this?

Initially, because you set an exemplary example, we must set an exemplary example to effect positive change in the world. It also conveys your appreciation for your employees despite their unique qualities.

As a business proprietor, you want to ensure that you conduct yourself legally, morally, and ethically. A high employee attrition rate harms an organization, and a diverse workforce possesses inherent value.

An instance of this is the educational background inquiry that appears on all job applications and is a prerequisite for the resume. Furthermore, numerous employers require a college degree as a prerequisite for employment. Sometimes, a master's or bachelor's degree is even mandatory.

Are individuals who lack a college degree truly stupid? Not in the least. Richard Branson, Bill Gates, Mark Zuckerberg, and Steve Jobs are not college graduates despite being among the wealthiest and most intelligent individuals alive today. At $27 billion, oil magnate Harold Hamm is the wealthiest individual in the country who has amassed a fortune without earning a college degree.

Maintaining the status quo may not be the most effective strategy today. In contemporary society, I believe individuals are aware that diverse parenting styles, educational backgrounds, and other factors can contribute novel and valuable perspectives to a business.

When managers recognize and promote equality and equity, employees are more inclined to develop professionally and make maximum contributions to the organization, as they will feel appreciated.

In addition to resources and support, equity also involves justice and parity in results. Organizations strive to identify and acknowledge unique requirements associated with demographic attributes (e.g., ethnicity, race, gender, and gender identity), impairments, and other relevant factors to promote workplace equity.

Several employers refused to engage individuals of a particular nationality, religion, or gender when I first began my professional career (and regrettably, this continues to be an issue).

Presently, applications inquire about the applicant's religion, age, sexual orientation, marital status, and educational attainment, among other things. Despite companies' adamant denials of discrimination and decision-making predicated on these factors, their possession of this information is currently obscure.

Similar to how it safeguards against discrimination on the grounds of race and gender, federal law also protects employees against such discrimination based on sexual orientation and gender identity. Companies should, therefore, be aware of their status.

# Contact A Mentor

Regardless of profession or career path, everyone requires direction, role models, and support. Obtaining all of that is most effectively accomplished through mentorship. In the past, mentoring was primarily the responsibility of parents who wished to impart their expertise to future generations. It is quite uncommon in the workplace of the twenty-first century. A mentor is particularly difficult to locate for those who pursue unconventional careers, such as entrepreneurship or artistic endeavors.

A mentor is an individual who can provide guidance, assistance, mentorship, and support in the pursuit of one's professional aspirations. An homage to Luke Skywalker by Yoda. Elements beyond a typical network connection distinguish a mentor-mentee relationship. It constitutes an enduring dedication and a profound investment in one's future.

In contrast to the brief introductions, business card exchanges, and phone calls that may characterize a typical network contact, your association with a mentor is expected to entail extended brunches and frequent visits to the mentor's office. Sometimes, a mentor occupies a position that mirrors your own and possesses the knowledge and networks necessary to direct you toward a comparable position. He or she is likely someone with whom you share uncanny excellent chemistry and will recount anecdotes from their journey toward achievement. A trustworthy mentor will also offer constructive criticism when necessary.

How do mentors operate?

In addition to assisting you in identifying your assets and weaknesses, a mentor can also guide you in cultivating success-oriented skills and formulating a strategic career trajectory. assist you in navigating company politics and culture, and provide information about the organization's key actors if the same company employs you and your mentor. You can also receive guidance from your mentor to resolve challenges in your professional life and at work. A mentor can offer a novel viewpoint—an alternative method of analyzing a given issue or problem. Ideas can be exchanged with a mentor. Seek out a mentoring relationship where the mentor assumes the role of a coach rather than an advisor and where alternative steps are suggested to aid in decision-making instead of providing explicit instructions. Your mentor should ideally inspire you to perform your best task.

Methods for Locating a Mentor

Determine whether a formal mentoring program is already established at your current place of employment, institution, or any other affiliated organization. Sometimes, personality assessments are administered to participants in these structured arrangements so that they may be matched with compatible mentors. Additional organizations have discovered that greater opportunities for discovery arise when mentors and mentees are extremely dissimilar.

To independently locate a mentor, identify an individual you respect and admire. You are not limited to selecting a mentor from within or without your place of employment; some individuals have multiple mentors. "Serial mentors," or individuals with whom one maintains a succession of brief-term relationships, can benefit certain individuals. Short-term mentoring relationships are defined by authors Devon Scheef and Beverly Kaye as "networking," a process that combines mentoring and networking and enables participants to give and receive in relationships where all parties are simultaneously teachers and learners. "You shall... impart your expertise and capabilities to others, acting as a mentor to many individuals," the authors state. In other words, numerous short-term learning teams are formed as each "mentworker" receives and imparts intellectual capacity to others.

Determine the qualities you desire in a mentor and the abilities you hope to acquire with the support of your mentor. Consider your objectives when selecting a mentor. Reflect upon the qualities that you would prefer to see in a mentor. You may wish to conduct some investigative research to ascertain the potential mentor's character traits. In what manner does he or she communicate? Solicit the perspectives of the prospective mentor's colleagues and subordinates.

Selecting a colleague who operates within the same functional domain as you and possesses similar values is advisable. Professional organizations within your industry can serve as valuable resources for advisors, regardless of whether they provide formal mentoring programs. Assess the situation by seeking guidance. Ensure that as much of yourself as possible is revealed. Because mentors are inclined to invest in individuals who reflect a small portion of themselves, it is ill-advised to approach a potential mentor while feeling hopeless or discouraged.

Having a mentor rather than your immediate superior is advisable, as the former may not be the most suitable person to discuss candidly career and workplace matters. Others benefit from peer mentors, whereas some mentees prefer an older, more experienced mentor at a higher organizational level so that they, too, may aspire to the highest echelons of the career hierarchy. Fast Company magazine features the experience of Lourdes Townsend, who participated in a program sponsored by her employer, Stride Rite, wherein she collaborated with twenty peer mentors. "I never thought about learning from someone on my level,"

Townsend asserts. "I often cast my gaze upwards two to four levels and pondered the necessary steps to ascend that level." However, those who are frequently confronted with the same challenges I am frequently possess the most effective resolutions.

As suggested by Townsend's experience, mentoring is occasionally carried out in groups. Women Unlimited, an initiative dedicated to advancing ambitious women, utilizes a framework whereby three mentees are paired with mentors.

HOW CHAPTER 2 EVOLVED THE CAPTAIN

"Leaders are created rather than born. And they are created through laborious effort, just like anything else. "And we must pay that price to accomplish any objective."

To address the age-old question, do leaders emerge from their social environments, or are they born leaders? Leadership is not a heritable characteristic that can be inherited via genetic means. Effective leadership techniques are acquired by observing one's social environment and utilizing resources (e.g., literature, mentors, parents).

Leadership involves an element of the relationship between a leader and a follower.1 Leadership is, from a technical standpoint, a strategic competency.2 Effective leadership requires surmounting challenges and imparting this understanding to others. Proficient leaders can exert control over others and inspire in them a feeling of self-assurance.3 Although the definitions above delineate the concept of leadership and what constitutes a leader, I maintain the opinion that merely defining a leader is tantamount to confining them to a particular cage. The strongest leaders, in my opinion, do not operate in any category. The essence of leadership is not expressed in words but rather in deeds and the opinions of others. One does not define oneself as a leader; instead, the perception of others influences one's development into a leader. Therefore, instead of a written definition of leadership, I shall furnish you with tools and competencies that will enable you to conduct yourself in a manner that merits the designation of a leader among your team members or followers, as I shall henceforth refer to them.

It was once said to me that assuming the role of a supervisor over others is equivalent to assuming the role of the ship's commander. You must guide your crew in the appropriate course of action. This is no way to approach this power casually. You acquire the ability to exert influence over individuals who regard you as a source of guidance and trust. The ability to command or supervise many individuals should never be considered a given. You are now tasked with making difficult decisions impacting every team member. Demonstrate self-assurance and maneuver that vessel in any desired course.

Being the ship's commander does not entail perpetual supervision of the crew. Demonstrating to the crew that no task is too minor and engaging in physical labor together effectively fosters a sense of assurance among them regarding their leader. This mantra was imparted to me rather early on in life. An individual occupying a much higher position in the leadership hierarchy than myself, the camp director, consistently performed menial tasks such as cooking, delivering food, cleaning restrooms, and performing acrobatic dances on stage, and required assistance with daily operations. Being a leader does not absolve oneself of the responsibility to be present at the forefront.

Establishing oneself as a leader by exhibiting the capability and willingness to participate in the team's daily operations rather than imposing authority on them is a crucial preliminary measure in cultivating the confidence and esteem of those who have faith in one's judgment. You will also avoid developing into a dictatorial leader as a result. Gaining an appreciation for the potency of humility is imperative for individuals assuming leadership positions to prevent the emergence of authoritarian leadership. This type of leader considers themselves superior to those who perform menial tasks and looks down upon them. Although delegation has benefits, imposing all obligations on your team will erode confidence in your leadership capabilities.

Being selected as a team commander signifies that you can guide your group to extraordinary achievements. Without a shadow of a doubt, you are in this position for a reason; however, you must never allow this authority to control you. Maintain your humility and confidence in yourself.

A susceptibility

Consider for a moment what it means to be vulnerable. What is the definition of vulnerability? Have you considered your feelings regarding being vulnerable and exposed? Numerous individuals perceive vulnerability in this manner. I request you remove that perspective from your mind and dispose of it. True vulnerability is among the most courageous demonstrations a leader can bestow upon his or her team.

In the context of this guide, I intend to cite Brené Brown's work and her book Dare to Lead 5 to explain and elaborate on the necessity of vulnerability for all exceptional leaders. It is essential to view vulnerability as a virtue rather than a weakness. Vulnerability is a state in which one feels susceptible to physical or emotional damage, thereby subjecting oneself to danger and unpredictability. However, why is that regarded negatively? Reflect upon the most exceptional leaders of all time, such as Martin Luther King Jr., Winston Churchill, Eleanor Roosevelt, and even the most accomplished members of your social circle. Everyone exposed themselves to potential danger, oblivious to the result. Certainly horrifying, but you should embrace it. The quality of vulnerability is intrinsic to bravery, and it facilitates personal development. Bear in mind that "to feel is to be vulnerable." "Being vulnerable to the point of weakness is tantamount to perceiving emotion as weakness."6

Please consider the following when you consider vulnerability:

Willingness to seek assistance

Exhibiting empathy

Displaying fortitude

Having an open mind toward new ideas

Daily, the most exceptional leaders confront unpredictability and danger; they relish their susceptibility to execute audacious decisions. A critical ability that contributes to the success of exceptional leaders is vulnerability.

Regarding Vision

How can one follow an individual who lacks a distinct vision? How can one be expected to contribute to a team's pursuit of a vision, objective, or purpose without prior knowledge of said entity or even the existence thereof? In the absence of vision, teams labor aimlessly. Effective leaders possess a distinct vision and impart that vision to their team members. Individuals determine their loyalty according to the leader's vision and their confidence in that leader's ability to execute it.7

However, exceptional leaders' perpetual readiness to reassess and modify their vision distinguishes them.8 Alter it if you have the foresight to recognize that something is malfunctioning. By adjusting one's vision, one can persevere and succeed. Adhering strictly to your initial vision may result in a detour and an inability to achieve the desired outcome. In addition, vision is a critical component of leading from behind.

## A PERSPECTIVE DURATION

Leveraging Diverse Vantage Points to Guide Leadership Priorities

In times of crisis, perspective is vital.

During our discussion of the Deepwater Horizon crisis, I expressed a few inquiries regarding the extensive scope of the situation. What perspective might Hyundai Heavy Engineering, BP, and Transocean executives have on this crisis? Predictably, the incident consumed their attention—not just for several days, but for months. Although these leaders held a singular, crucial viewpoint regarding the crisis, it was not the only one that held significance.

It is evident from research and personal experience that organizational leadership teams must address the concerns of other stakeholders, who hold alternative viewpoints and rely on leadership for guidance, information, and assurance that their interests will be safeguarded. These concerns may be substantial and will necessitate focus— occasionally immediate and occasionally nearly continuous focus—during a critical situation.

A further essential element of crisis leadership is the difficulty leaders encounter due to the constrained time and resources available amid a crisis. How will leaders, constrained by time and resources, effectively attend to every stakeholder's concerns affected by a crisis? Sometimes, it is impossible to accomplish everything you know you should (e.g., press conferences, private meetings, phone conversations, and emails) due to a lack of available time, personnel, or financial resources. To navigate a crisis successfully, leaders must involve all their stakeholder groups. However, due to time constraints, particularly at the onset of a crisis, they must make challenging concessions, deciding which stakeholders to address initially and in what manner, while recognizing that while certain stakeholders will receive immediate attention, others will be relegated to lower priority status. How should crisis leaders approach this obstacle? A little bit of pre-planning can be extremely useful at this point. Strategically anticipating specific types of crises can assist leaders with significant consequences in determining which stakeholder groups are most susceptible to particular scenarios. However, according to research, very few organizations try to do so. Therefore, we will conduct a brief exercise to provide you with some practice in identifying the main stakeholder groups affected by various types of crises. In the subsequent sections, please reflect on four distinct real-life crisis scenarios, perform a rapid evaluation of the essence of the crisis, and identify the stakeholder groups with active involvement you deem most imperative.

# Real-World Crises, Optimal For Quarterbacking On Monday Mornings

While contemplating the subsequent scenarios, most of which will be acquainted with you, please jog your mind over a few essential inquiries for each.

To begin, is the occurrence consistent with our predefined criteria for a crisis? ("A situation or period characterized by instability or criticality, wherein a significant shift is imminent, particularly one that carries the clear potential for an extremely unfavorable consequence.") If so, then time and effort from the executive should be devoted to the event.

Furthermore, which stakeholder groups will be substantially affected by the event, and which of these groups ought to be designated as "priority stakeholders" by the leadership team? Once more, although it is precise to assert that every stakeholder group will experience some degree of repercussion from an organizational crisis and warrants your consideration at some point, in practice, specific crises will have a more pronounced effect on particular stakeholder groups. As a high-stakes leader, it will be your responsibility to ascertain which of these groups demands the most of your time and which merits it immediately rather than later.

Thirdly, what are the wants and needs of these priority stakeholders that require my attention? True crisis leadership rock stars are those who can respond and act upon this third question with the utmost importance.

Apply the responses to the following three scenarios to the three queries.

Chapter 2: Recognize the Present Circumstances

What is occurring?

Before progressing toward improving current affairs, you must determine what is and is not functioning.

Examine both the hard and emotional data.

Hard data consists of numerical values. The figures provide insight regarding the economy, market share, sales, expenses, profit, and turnover. Moreover, it is advantageous to comprehend the significant tendencies. Future events can also be predicted using numbers.

The passive data provides an alternative account. It assesses emotions, frustrations, anxieties, and energy levels among individuals. Consider the dynamic component of the situation.

Both categories of data offer significant insights into the present circumstances.

Implement a Course of Action

Leave your office and engage in conversation with others. Inquire extensively and generate a multitude of observations. Determine how individuals allocate their time and resources. Which procedures are automatable?

What are individuals' greatest frustrations, assets, weaknesses, and successes?

How well do individuals concur on a shared set of objectives and strategies? To what extent is collaboration prevalent across the entire organization?

Solicit input from various stakeholders, such as suppliers, customers, employees, managers, stockholders, and external consultants. One might possess a unique perspective on reality.

In conclusion, integrate every component to comprehensively depict the present circumstances. Which are several significant themes and patterns?

Erroneous Perspective on Reality

Certain leaders err in their assessment of the present circumstance for an assortment of reasons, which include the following:

Avoidance is the reluctance to uncover unpleasant issues for fear that doing so will reflect poorly on one.

Blind areas are defined as having a distorted perception of particular aspects of one's operation and oneself. They frequently perceive their performance to be considerably superior to its true caliber.

Insufficient Observation— hastening to conclusions based on a restricted amount of data collection.

Neglecting the importance—By neglecting the significance of specific metrics.

Focusing exclusively on the information that corroborates one's viewpoint constitutes selective listening.

Yes, People—Caritasones who actively encourage the dissemination of positive information and offer an optimistic perspective on negative ones.

Prevent falling prey to these pitfalls.

Compel oneself to be curious and receptive to diverse perspectives.

Encourage individuals to voice their opinions and present all relevant, positive and negative information.

Ascertain the critical concrete data that warrants inclusion in the analysis.

Advocate for the devil's cause. Question prevailing assumptions.

Observe adequately to discern recurring patterns of behavior.

In summary, comprehending the present circumstances enables one to discern what functions effectively while recognizing the necessity and feasibility of modifications.

Figure Four in Chapter Four

The Superhero's Method of Success

A short while ago, the CEO of a mid-sized technology company undergoing "market transformations" summoned me to a dire situation. In business jargon, this statement can be roughly translated as "HELP! "Our heads are being bashed in." They had initiated a significant initiative to revitalize competitiveness several months prior. They believed that work followed schedule, established plans, and assembled teams. Each time the high-ranking individual inquired about the project's progress, the response consisted of an upbeat "Fine!" or "Good!" These phrases mean, "I'm not sure, but I'm overwhelmed, and no one is shouting, so I suppose it can wait a while."

As deadlines passed, attitudes and status reports progressively deteriorated. Upon transforming "need a little more time" into "OMG!" the supervisor issued a warning and requested assistance. Unfortunately, my arrival was too late; this superhero flew through the unreserved class. An extensive energy-squandering, justification-making, and finger-pointing (index first, then another) project meltdown was underway. (Argh!) Have you encountered a comparable circumstance? This is the superhero's signal to intervene and save the day in the movies. However, this is not Hollywood. Despite my sincere desire to identify with a gratifyingly cinematic, joyful ending, I cannot do so. The undertaking proved to be a catastrophe. The attempt failed. In reality, it had already failed long before I arrived, preceding the weeping, finger-pointing, and even the initial attempt. "How have you been?"

Projects falter at the outset, not at their conclusion.

During the later phases of a project, favorable decisions have been made, overlooked, or disregarded. Increasing the stage of a project's lifecycle revealed a greater variety of options. The dilemma is as follows: during the last days of a project, one has complete knowledge of what worked and what did not, which assumptions were accurate or incorrect, and what alternative approach could have been more effective; in fact, their vision is flawless! Unfortunately, time travel is not possible. Early in the undertaking, however, when the greatest number of options and alternatives are present, your vision is at its worst. You may have only a hazy notion of where you are headed, how you intend to get there, and what to anticipate.

In the final stages of a project, there are few remaining options and choices, and the majority of them have unfavorable outcomes:

● Abandon the endeavor and concede defeat ● Request additional time and funds (again) ● Commence a new endeavor with fresh personnel ● Employ alternative vendors ● Modify the project's scope ● Proclaim triumph with the hope that no one notices ● Revitalise one's resume

Your capacity to influence success diminishes significantly as the project life cycle advances. Precise decisions must be reached in the beginning when comprehension is limited; this is the perpetual dilemma of the project planner. Scale and alter your process model to the specific requirements of each project for optimal results. For instance, a small, low-risk endeavor necessitates fewer organization, supervision, and evaluation measures compared to a sizable, high-risk, or complex undertaking.

In 1916, the prodigious management expert Henri Fayol articulated, "Established principles ought to be regarded as malleable, adaptable to any circumstance. The manager is responsible for effectively utilizing them, an intricate skill that demands intellect, practical experience, and, above all else, a keen sense of proportions. Despite my sincere desire to do otherwise, the process does not allow us to perceive the future. However, it accomplishes the bare minimum. An efficient project management process broadens, enhances, and focuses our existing knowledge, maintains the critical outcomes in crystal clear view, and illuminates our decisions brilliantly. By implementing an effective process, one can advance a project at an unprecedented rate and with enhanced safety. Rely on your CAPE!

Avoid allowing the process paradigm to control you.

Strategies for Taking Charge of Failing Projects

Averted difficulties can only be avoided with the foresight that an efficient process model provides if one dislikes stalled initiatives. To be candid, I abhor troubled endeavors. I strive to avoid them, and I recommend that you do the same. Nevertheless, all professionals who appreciate the convenience of indoor environments and regular meals must eventually confront a challenging project that may involve irate colleagues, condescending stakeholders, and frustrating suppliers. As an illustration, I undertook the reversal task introduced at the outset of this chapter. Despite being aware of the dangerous nature of the undertaking, I possessed an undisclosed advantage: the principals also placed their trust in me. As detailed below, they consented to my "never accept another person's project mess unless essential." Ultimately, we (and I do mean we; this was a triumph of the entire team) achieved success, which fortified the organization. If you ever find yourself in a comparable predicament, the following delineates my approach to resolving projects:

● Preserve the resources at your disposal. Document any advancements, deliverables, or knowledge acquired. Even if the only tangible result is knowing what not to do, that is still progress. Successfully advancing to the subsequent phase is contingent upon the main stakeholders avoking defeat at the hands of the present approach.

Eliminate the endeavor. Delaying resolution results in squandering scarce resources, misinforming the project team, and instilling unrealistic expectations among the principal stakeholders. Maintaining this project in progress will inevitably drain the energy of the project team and impede their ability to progress to the subsequent phase. This is a grim phase, but it is impossible to completely outrun a zombie.

● Rescue the populace. The team did not create this chaos. The organization created this muddled disaster due to a lack of process, insufficient stakeholder participation, overconfidence, and many other fundamental flaws. This group has undoubtedly acquired valuable insights that have proven to be detrimental, or they will be more receptive to an improved strategy. Retaining and treating them respectfully will probably elicit renewed determination and genuine engagement. By preserving lives, your organization can gain insights for which you have already incurred expenses. Lastly, and arguably most significantly, how individuals are regarded during such circumstances establishes the foundation for future enterprise staffing and collaboration.

❖❖❖ Commence again. Apply the framework, self-control, and advantages resulting from utilizing an efficient project management procedure this time.

# Fundamental Communication Abilities

Listening actively is the key to comprehension.

Communication is the foundation of human interaction, analogous to the progressive development of our comprehension of diverse topics throughout history. Like the necessity of a varied repertoire of abilities to navigate the intricacies of contemporary work settings, the value of exceptional interpersonal skills also applies to the efficient administration of diverse personalities in the modern workplace. In the contemporary business environment, achievement is contingent not solely on personal aptitudes but also on superiors, clients, and colleagues.

Analogous to the development of numerous academic disciplines, the application of communication has evolved from mere fundamental exchanges to a greater emphasis on its capacity to revolutionize professional engagements. Similar to how progress in various fields strives to enhance the standard of living, achieving proficiency in communication skills entails fostering collaborations that elevate the workplace and contribute to developing significant professional connections.

Engaged Listening

Active listening is considered to be a fundamental pillar within the realm of critical communication abilities. This activity surpasses ordinary auditory reception; it necessitates complete involvement with the speaker's discourse, comprehension of their viewpoint, and affirmation of their emotions. Professionals ought to recognize the importance of active listening to better comprehend their colleagues' perspectives and establish more robust relationships.

The Influence of Active Listening on Interpersonal Connections

Active listening functions as a protective barrier against the adverse outcomes arising from misunderstandings, conflicts, and disrupted relationships that may arise due to inadequate communication within a team. Fostering relationships is accomplished by displaying respect, empathy, and honesty. Acknowledging the indicators of active listening—which include sustaining visual engagement, seeking clarification through inquiries, and offering reflective replies—is critical for fostering an atmosphere conducive to effective communication.

Development of Active Listening

To proficiently apply active listening in professional contexts, it is critical to develop a mindful mindset. To illustrate their dedication to comprehension, professionals may employ strategies including paraphrasing, summarizing, and abstaining from interruptions.

Methods for Successful Implementation

To integrate active listening into communication dynamics effectively, one must do so deliberately and consistently. Professionals can employ various strategies, including relegating distractions, maintaining an open posture, and devoting concentrated time to discussions. By fostering an environment in which coworkers feel acknowledged and appreciated, improving the caliber of communication and positively contributing to a more efficient and cohesive workplace is feasible.

Training in Assertiveness: Discovering Your Voice

In a manner analogous to the evolution of viewpoints in numerous disciplines, our comprehension of the function of communication has progressed throughout history. Like maintaining a well-balanced diet is critical for averting deficiencies and associated health conditions, developing exceptional interpersonal skills enables one to effectively navigate the unique dynamics of the contemporary workplace. In the contemporary business environment, achievement extends beyond individual proficiencies to include the capacity to engage in effective communication with superiors, clients, and colleagues.

In tandem with the development of numerous academic fields, the examination of communication has progressed from focusing on simple dialogue to emphasizing the profound impact that proficient interaction can have. Similar to how progress in various domains aims to improve the standard of living, attaining proficiency in communication skills necessitates cultivating partnerships that elevate the workplace and nurture significant professional connections.

As one of several critical communication skills, assertiveness training is indispensable. This activity entails expressing one's thoughts, emotions and needs with assurance while demonstrating regard for the perspectives of others. In a manner analogous to how functional approaches can optimize health, professionals must acknowledge assertiveness training to cultivate healthier communication dynamics and facilitate self-expression.

Analogous to how harmful components in one's diet can hurt overall health, a lack of assertiveness in communication can result in misinterpretations, inappropriate expectations, and discord among team members. By encouraging candid and transparent communication, assertiveness fosters stronger relationships and acts as a buffer against these negative effects. Establishing clear boundaries, engaging in active listening, and demonstrating assertive behaviors are critical to fostering an atmosphere that promotes productive and respectful communication.

To cultivate assertiveness effectively, one must adopt a holistic approach to communication. Akin to the integration of various components to achieve comprehensive wellness, fostering assertive behaviors requires an appreciation for one's expression and the viewpoints of others. To enhance assertive communication abilities, professionals may utilize methods such as employing "I" statements to articulate thoughts, employing direct communication to communicate requirements, and engaging in role-playing scenarios.

The deliberate incorporation of assertiveness into communication dynamics requires skill, practice, and intention. Proficient individuals may utilize tactics such as developing introspection, practicing dialogues, and soliciting constructive criticism to hone their assertive communication skills. Individuals can enhance the equilibrium and efficiency of the workplace by cultivating a culture that prioritizes candid and courteous discourse.

## 1. A Philosophical Consideration of Richness

Although everyone desires to be wealthy, only a minority achieve that status during their lifetimes. Although it is not a criminal offense to be born into poverty, failing to maximize one's potential and dying in poverty is undoubtedly a criminal offense. Acquiring material wealth and money are not the only components of wealth. It is about the transformation of an individual into a millionaire. I first profoundly understood the requirements for achieving wealth in 2010. I paid a visit to my relative in Chennai. He asked me, "Are you proficient in generating income and fostering its growth?" I was unable to respond to his inquiry.

"Do you know the formula for simple interest?" he inquired. I responded affirmatively. Subsequently, he inquired which term is the most critical component of the simple interest formula. Was it the principal, the interest rate, or the time the funds were invested? I pondered for some time without arriving at a definitive response. He informed me that the answer is the length of time an investor can hold onto their funds. According to Albert Einstein, compound interest is the greatest force in the universe. To better understand finance and wealth, my uncle suggested I read Rich Dad and Poor Dad.

I promptly procured the book and commenced reading it. The profound insights it imparted revolutionized my comprehension of wealth and affluence. Subsequently, I delved into works such as "Secrets of Self-Made Millionaires," and "Science of Getting Rich" while also researching the lives of affluent individuals, including Bill Gates, Warren Buffet, and the Talas. The following are the fundamental distinctions between the wealthy and the impoverished:

1. The poor work for their money, while the wealthy put their money to work for them. However, once they do, they spend more than they earn on luxuries and unnecessary items, and they take out loans they must repay for the rest of their lives. On the other hand, the wealthy begin by accumulating financial assets such as land, gold, smart investments, financial knowledge, and bookwriting.

2. Constantly increase donations: Individuals of genuine affluence consistently allocate a greater portion of their wealth to charitable endeavors and good causes. The golden rule of wealth posits that one should increase their contributions proportionately to their gains; wealth will be returned to them in multiples of the sum donated. Bill Gates, who has accumulated a personal fortune of $65 billion over an extended period, has dedicated most of

his wealth to charitable purposes, aiming to eradicate poverty and enhance healthcare for the impoverished.

3. Superior service and dedication to excellence: Napoleon Hill once said, "One day, you will be compensated significantly more than you currently do." Constantly deliver superior service, perform outstanding work, and exceed customers' expectations. Developing these qualities will ultimately yield substantial financial returns.

4. Reliance on a secondary source of income: It is imprudent to rely solely on one source of income. Diversify your sources of income at all times. Invest to establish a secondary source. Warren Buffet said, "Never test the river's depth with both feet. Do not put all the eggs in the same basket". True prosperity consists of earnings from all sources besides one's primary source of income.

5. Appreciation and a positive mindset: Napoleon Hill once said, "Anything the mind can conceive, it can attain." Acquiring wealth requires unwavering self-confidence and a positive mindset. Individuals who possess an attitude of gratitude consistently prosper in their pursuit of wealth. By counting their blessings, you will understand that they extend infinitely.

6. Honesty: In the same vein, Warren Buffett advises, "Honesty is a pricey gift; do not expect it from those who are cheap." A positive reputation increases the likelihood that others will trust you and offer you more advantageous opportunities.

7. Seek counsel from knowledgeable individuals: To attain wealth, peruse the counsel of financially successful individuals. One notable attribute of accomplished individuals is their perpetual willingness to impart their wisdom and experience to those

approaching them for guidance. By imitating the actions of successful individuals, one is assured of attaining success.

According to research, the average individual must wait twenty-two years after deciding to become a millionaire before they can achieve that status. A few exceptions to this norm exist at all times. A recent study revealed that eighty individuals possess fifty percent of the world's riches. We are all visited by the Goddess of Wealth at some point. However, she only associates with individuals who respect affluence and can capitalize on opportunities.

First Chapter

Leadership at the Peak Performance Level

The 1990s marked the height of the Chicago Bulls basketball program. The team consistently showcased remarkable and intricate demonstrations of basketball theatrics in every contest. The nationwide audience was mesmerized by spinning leaps, extraordinary dunks, and precise long shots. Even those who had no interest in basketball relished watching them compete. Due to their immense popularity, numerous Chicago Bulls players accompanied celebrities on evening talk shows, political balls, and sports programs. Everyone adored them, and Michael Jordan's name became a household name.

Upon his initial day of service with the Chicago Bulls, Michael Jordan promptly established himself as a player of unparalleled caliber. College and high school athletes were eager to replicate his remarkable art, which included slam dunks from the free throw line, extraordinary leaps, and aggressive ball control. Even though spectators eagerly awaited Michael Jordan to demonstrate his astounding basketball prowess further and further, the majority of individuals were oblivious to the true nature of the situation occurring behind the scenes.

Michael Jordan needed a selection by Scottie Pippen, a low-post screen by Bill Cartwright, or even a clear-out by Horace Grant to accomplish his goals. Not to detract from Michael's abilities, he could not have accomplished him without these individuals performing their duties.

Even though Michael Jordan attained legendary status and the Chicago Bulls won three consecutive NBA Championships, it is important to remember that seven arduous years of planning and tens of thousands of hours of practice were required to get them there. This extraordinary group and its lead player did not begin at the epitome of greatness. They were required to put in effort to reach their destination.

Like any other group, they had to develop the confidence to follow their coach's unconventional practice techniques. They were required to determine their group's purpose, form a cohesive unit, identify one another's assets and weaknesses, and master the art of synergistic collaboration. They subsequently entered the zone of optimum performance. They retained their championship status for three consecutive years, undefeated.

It would be fantastic if you could advocate for a similar high-performing team at your place of employment. You simply release them onto the office floor, and they immediately begin slamming project after project to the ground, generating documentation as if time were no object and, ultimately, impressing you and every other upper-level supervisor with their skill and expertise in their respective roles.

You could be amused as you consider your team performing these actions. It may appear absurd as you survey your current work environment and resources, but I urge you to at least consider the advice presented in this book. I guarantee that by applying the principles outlined in this book, you will uncover a trajectory that can ultimately result in a high-performing team that was previously inconceivable.

Over the last two decades, I have had the honor of instructing thousands of managers and executives from large and small organizations across the nation. The principles that I impart to various audiences, including senior executives at the Department of Agriculture, sales managers at AT&T, and shoe sales managers at local department stores, are documented in this book. They are a synthesis of my personal experience and the research and experiences of numerous great leaders I have examined for the past three decades.

Consequently, many of the managers and leaders under my guidance have conveyed how these principles have significantly benefited their professional development in management and leadership. These ideas synthesize experience, wisdom, and common sense; they are based on the counsel of great leaders and numerous eternal truths that can be discovered in the Bible, business, and daily life.

Simply put, this literature serves a purpose! My objective is to assist you in developing into a peak-performance leader capable of building, training, and leading a high-performing team that completes tasks with greater speed and efficiency. Without a doubt, you will also desire that as a leader, management, or supervisor!

The truth is that it is possible! You have already demonstrated that you are an individual of optimum performance. You have already demonstrated your abilities and aptitudes to those in positions of authority, be they pastor, manager, supervisor, or both. They have been persuaded of your superiority over your colleagues. You have demonstrated your capability, dependability, and competence. You are an individual who excels at optimum performance, which is precisely what is required to begin!

To construct a peak performance team in the twenty-first century, one must know such a team's characteristics and functioning principles. Comprehending these concepts and having a well-defined objective is already half the battle.

# These Are Required To Lead.

Have you ever attended a staff meeting where the manager was the only one who spoke? Brendon posed that as his challenge.

Brendon held a weekly meeting with his staff. After reviewing the itinerary each time, he would discuss departmental and corporate updates. He would request feedback and solicit the team's opinion at some juncture. This did not occur.

Brendon desired to participate in a constructive discourse. After identifying what was and was not functioning, the group would devise a solution. Brendon would subsequently clarify that he believed this to be the behavior of healthy teams. They would discuss, resolve, debate, and reach an agreement. In Brendon's opinion, these actions would facilitate their development into a high-performing unit.

Brendon's reality, sadly, was different. Brendon would inquire about the participants' perspectives to commence this dialogue, including evaluating the team's recent task mastery. Unavoidably, two behavioral patterns emerged within the team. The vast majority of the time, nobody would speak. After minutes of silence, Brendon would alter the subject and transition to another one.

Occasional remarks would be made. Brendon's optimism would momentarily increase. Brendon would encourage others to participate in the discussion following his contribution. Conversely, the group would avert their gaze towards their notepads or squirm. Everyone appeared uneasy, Brendon included.

Brendon was aware of his need for assistance. I came to three conclusions after Brendon answered a few questions I had him pose after he disclosed his issue. Despite his extensive knowledge of the business and his organization, Brendon never gave much thought to leadership. Furthermore, Brendon possessed an earnest desire to realize his aspiration of spearheading a formidable team. Thirdly, Brendon unsuccessfully attempted to inspire his team with various strategies. I deduced from these observations the factors that hindered Brendon's ability to lead effectively.

Before elaborating, it is necessary to acquire some knowledge regarding Brendon.

Brendon worked as a programmer for a technology development team of programmers before before assuming the team leader role. While operating autonomously, the team members sought advice from one another and exchanged programming insights.

Brendon primarily devoted countless hours to arduously debugging code. He discovered that the work was not only instructive but also gratifying. Brendon's labor yielded innovative resolutions, which he enthusiastically communicated to his teammates.

While conversing, Brendon was oblivious to his limited understanding of leadership. His understanding of leaders was derived from his engagements with administrators and managers. Although he spent most of his time with Breonna, his team manager, he adopted several of her leadership principles.

I inquired about Brendon's leadership methodology. He was forced to consider for the first time what leadership entails and his approach to it. Brendon had difficulty conveying to me the actions and motivations of Breonna and other managers who exemplified leadership.

When I inquired how his teammates led, he could not comprehend or even consider the possibility that subordinates could lead effectively without managerial authority. The notion was unfamiliar to him.

Brendon encountered two factors that rendered leadership arduous. Brendon struggled to discern the managerial behaviors of Breonna and other managers from their leadership practices as he observed them.

Further, Brendon could not observe the guiding principles governing how managers led.

Regarding Brendon's predicament, it is possible to perceive the actions of an individual; however, the underlying motivations that drive said actions remain elusive. For this reason, it is challenging for criminal prosecutors to persuade juries to find an accused person guilty of first-degree homicide. Prosecutors would need to deduce intent to plot and carry out the act to accomplish this.

The formulation of leadership principles is even more challenging than determining why individuals lead as they do. It would be considerably simpler to comprehend the meaning of a principle by observing examples rather than identifying behavioral patterns that result in the formulation of principles that govern behavior in various contexts.

As I previously stated, leadership entails the application of our respective responsibilities. Led by principles is what we do. We can lead effectively if we can internalize leadership principles and apply them to various situations. As the adage goes, this is regrettably easier said than done.

One might inquire whether principles and values are synonymous. Values are often conflated with qualities, competencies, skills, abilities, and characteristics in my mind. Principles are less abstract than values. Instances of values include integrity, bravery, altruism, and modesty.

The particulars of principles are more precise. Several consultants I am acquainted with, for instance, adhere to the Add-Value Principle: provide clients with services that exceed their remuneration. Although clients benefit significantly from this principle, so do consultants.

The study of leadership values alone does not suffice to teach me about leadership due to the abstract nature of values. Even more difficult is the task of determining which leadership values exist. I discovered three lengthy discussions on LinkedIn in which participants were asked by their moderators to characterize leadership qualities. I compiled an inventory of every value that the members shared. After removing duplicates, I compiled a list of 270 qualities!

As an alternative to identifying values, I direct my attention towards principles.

Leadership principles are sufficiently general in scope to apply to various circumstances while remaining sufficiently general to delineate their application. Consider leadership principles our moral compass, which directs us through turbulent and tranquil waters. Leadership improves as the principles become more ingrained in one's being.

Although leadership principles are more practical than values or qualities, a comprehensive compilation of these principles is uncommon among leadership experts. To be fair to my case against using values, specialists do not concur on a universal set of principles. In the realm of leadership, ISO 9000 does not apply.

[15] To ascertain leadership principles for my book Nine Practices, I analyzed fourteen books authored by authorities on leadership. Except for one, every publication appeared in the twenty-first century. I extracted seven leadership principles from the works above. Each will be introduced in the following seven chapters.

The Significance of TPM in Alternative Product Management Positions:

Technical Product Management (TPM) is an elevated position within the product management domain that integrates product strategy and implementation with technical proficiency. Although there are numerous product management positions, TPM is distinguished from the rest by its distinctive benefits and value. This section will examine the comparative value of TPM concerning alternative product management positions.

**Technical Proficiency:** An essential factor distinguishing TPM is its profound technical expertise. Professionals in Technology Project Management (TPM) generally possess a technical or engineering background, which empowers them to comprehend intricate technical principles, facilitate effective communication with engineers, and serve as liaisons between technical groups and other interested parties. Such technical knowledge enables TPMs to make well-informed judgments, evaluate viability, and efficiently rank product prerequisites, fostering a harmonious connection between technical capabilities and business goals.

**Management of the Entire Product Lifecycle:** TPMs participate in each phase of the product lifecycle, beginning with requirements collection and ideation and continuing through launch and post-launch optimization. Their responsibilities include:

Ensuring successful product delivery by conducting market research.

Defining product requirements.

Aligning product strategy with business objectives.

They also collaborate closely with engineering, design, and other cross-functional teams. TPMs gain a comprehensive understanding of product management by being involved from beginning to end, which empowers them to make well-informed decisions and propel the product's success.

TPMs demonstrate exceptional proficiency in effectively administering various stakeholders, encompassing engineering teams, designers, executives, customers, and users. Successful product delivery is contingent upon their capacity to collaborate with cross-functional teams, resolve gaps between technical and non-technical stakeholders, and communicate technical requirements effectively. TPMs appreciate the perspectives and requirements of various stakeholders and can balance competing priorities in a manner that promotes consensus and alignment regarding product decisions.

An In-Depth Knowledge of Technical Constraints and Considerations TPMs have an extensive knowledge of technical constraints and considerations. Proficient in identifying potential hazards, evaluating feasibility, and negotiating compromises to attain the intended product results. TPMs can manage expectations, develop practical product roadmaps, and guarantee that products are developed within technical limitations while satisfying customer requirements and business objectives with this technical insight.

**Comparing the Technical and Business Worlds:** TPMs are an intermediary between the technical and business domains. They can convey technical complexities to non-technical stakeholders and translate business objectives into technical requirements. Due to their distinctive abilities, TPMs can guarantee that product strategies are based on technical capabilities, market demands, and business objectives. They integrate the most advantageous aspects of both realms, fostering innovation and producing goods that fulfill customers' requirements, all while creating value for the organization.

TPMs possess extensive knowledge and experience with Agile methodologies and practices, which empowers them to facilitate streamlined and iterative processes for product development. They promote an environment that values ongoing education, flexibility, and cooperation, cultivating a climate of invention and advancement. TPMs prioritize features, conduct iterative testing, collect feedback, and make data-driven decisions by Agile principles; this expedites time-to-market and improves customer satisfaction.

TPMs provide distinct advantages over other product management positions by their technical proficiency, active participation throughout the entire product lifecycle, proficient management of stakeholders, comprehension of technical limitations, ability to connect the business and technical sectors, and agile methodology.

Project management (TPM) specialists are of utmost importance in guaranteeing that products are in harmony with the technical capacities and business goals, producing favorable product results and propelling the organization's achievement. Their proficiency in managing through the intricate convergence of technology and business renders them indispensable personnel for any product-oriented organization.

# Selecting The Optimal Leadership Coach

In light of the third phase of the Industrial Revolution and changes in human resources, organizations favored coaching leaders. In the end, Lenovo Group, which has the most impressive resume in history, will implement coaching-style leadership.

As a result of the third phase of the industrial revolution, enterprise organizations are becoming more networked, and societal structures are transforming. Most employees eventually adopt a self-emphasis on the 80–90 employees following the pursuit of independence. Coaching-style executives have garnered significant attention from the business community nationwide and have been recognized as one of the top ten management practices of the year. The abovementioned subject was addressed in the July 2007 edition of "The World Manager" under "Coaching-Style

Leadership." He reasoned, "My words determine the command-based leadership style." Style leadership resembles me. Relational leaders assert that visionary leadership is carried out in collaboration with someone like you.

Collaborating with our organization, Phil's team considered various leadership styles and implemented a five-step procedure; the particular stages are outlined below. They are all "timely rain" for any organization interested in developing algorithmic models for leadership development.

1. Choose an Evaluation Instrument

Organizations require a leadership-type assessment instrument before implementing a personalized leadership development program. Following this, a portion, if not the entirety, of the leadership development material is screened and distributed to the relevant leaders.

Organizations may develop their personality criteria or utilize those of others, such as the Myers-Briggs, DISC, or Herman's Brain Strengths Scale. We have developed algorithms in StandOut programs, our online leadership qualifier assessment tool, according to the job requirements. StandOut is a scenario judgment test application that requests participants to indicate their anticipated response to a given sequence of situations. Our evaluations, as opposed to those that require candidates to rate a variety of characteristics, center on the behavior itself to more accurately reflect how others perceive individuals. Following an investigation into over 430,000 individuals whose subsequent performance was monitored, we formulated the StandOut program.

categories of behaviors prevalent among interviewees and referred to as "superior qualities." They symbolize the most prevalent way personal qualities converge and coalesce upon these particular leaders.

2. Assess Effective Leadership

Under the service-oriented Hilton brand, we employed the StandOut methodology on 150 highest-performing managers, representing the top 10%. As a consequence, in contrast to the formulaic leadership development model, we discovered that most of these nine traits were possessed by leaders rather than one or two that are universally shared. The model is not exceptional: we discovered that the leadership qualities exhibited by principals of the National Association of Independent Schools and Kohl's are comparable and that Habitat for Humanity's leadership qualities are identical. We discovered some of the most distinguished leaders in each category at Hilton, so we began to ascertain precisely what characteristics distinguished them.

3 Interview Various Leaders

Despite achieving comparable success levels, leaders with distinct strengths and qualities employ divergent leadership styles. As per Diana, the proprietor of Hampton Inn & Suites located in Pennsylvania, using an emblem to symbolize the desired behaviors and attitudes of her staff and unite them is crucial. Because "you will not make any progress if you do not stretch your neck out," she selects a turtle as her mascot. She emphasized the significance of imbuing work with "personality and objectives." It's no surprise that she would say so, given that her StandOut results indicate she has a knack for inspiring others and a propensity to generate drama, excitement, and energy.

Consideration of Experience versus Knowledge in Chapter 6

I want you to find this book extremely experiential and practical. Each individual appears to have amassed substantial knowledge, which is only marginally beneficial until it can be effectively implemented in practical, day-to-day circumstances. Comparing the ability to prepare biryani and the experience of serving it to others and witnessing their delight are disparate experiences.

Therefore, consider practicing whatever you perceive in this book in the real world. This is what the distinction "consider" entails.

The true test would be whether you can incorporate each of the various distinctions and concepts you master into practical, everyday situations. In my programs and public speaking, I have always insisted that individuals put the suggestion into practice, if only temporarily, and then report back to me on the changes that it has precipitated.

I strongly advise you to follow suit as you peruse this literary work. Individuals have reported experiencing miraculous events since they began incorporating each distinction into their lives.

Considering something is comparable to perusing an assortment of garments in a clothing store. At the same time, they are suspended in a row, and you approach each garment individually, engaging in tactile and tactile exploration. You select the blouse in the desired color. You do not purchase it at the invoicing counter immediately, correct? Are you? You visit a trial chamber where you attempt on the shirt. You might also consider showing it to family or friends you typically accompany shopping. You subsequently make a purchase decision based on your experience wearing and displaying the item.

It is highly recommended that you do so about the various tools, concepts, and distinctions examined in this discourse. Should you prefer to retain them, then do so. If not, you will discard them. Utilize whatever you desire to the fullest extent. Embrace it. Establish it as your own through consistent application in your daily existence.

Automotive Maintenance

Because consumer lives are at stake, the automotive industry functions most effectively under autocratic leadership, much like the airline industry. Although land vehicle collisions are generally less fatal than airplane crashes, passengers and bystanders remain at risk when manufacturing processes and policies about safety are not followed. As an illustration, the activation of airbags in automobiles is contingent upon impact sensitivity, which is determined through rigorous protocol adherence and accident dummy testing. Violators of any component of this protocol run the risk of impeding the intended deployment of the bag, which could result in severe injuries or fatalities to the driver or occupants. Autocratic leaders are considered the most effective automotive managers because they restrict deviations from established procedures in response to this type of hazard.

You have acquired knowledge regarding the benefits of autocratic leadership and the industries and organizations that benefit most from its implementation. As the majority of individuals would anticipate, this style of leadership is not without its drawbacks. This brings us to the following section, which elaborates on the drawbacks associated with autocratic leaders.

There are disadvantages.

Some link the term "autocratic" with pessimistic notions. They perceive autocratic leaders as tyrannical dictators who pronounce themselves as the preeminent authorities on all matters within their sphere of influence and never listen to dissenting opinions. As the benefits section explicitly states, this cannot be the case. Autocratic leaders have contributed to the expansion and success of numerous categories of organizations. Notwithstanding this, this style of leadership is not without its significant drawbacks. Notably, the drawbacks, as mentioned earlier, arise from the very elements that contribute to the benefits—rigid organization and unwavering compliance with protocols and guidelines. Nevertheless, the subsequent points delineate several prevalent drawbacks associated with autocratic leadership:

The practice of micromanagement

Probably the most widely recognized drawback of autocratic rule is this. Thorough observation is maintained to ensure structure preservation; control is paramount. In the military, this management style is tolerated and encouraged; however, it may prove harmful in the business world. It has been observed that the management strategies of autocratic business executives can backfire if they descend into micromanagement. Typically, this occurs when they:

Make all significant decisions independently of others' input.

Implement an extensive array of workplace policies and procedures

Remain steadfast in your commitment to a plan once it has been executed.

Before relying on information provided by others, verify its accuracy.

Notably, even innovative leaders can micromanage when they implement an autocratic management style. Although one might assume that creativity is limitless, this notion is shattered when those in authority attempt to exert an excessive amount of control. This process is exemplified by the renowned creator of Saturday Night Live, Lorne Michaels, who insists that all things have impassable boundaries. Some of his former employees have been offended by his conviction that creativity is impossible without limits. They disliked having their ideas restricted or regulated, and Michaels' efforts to do so gave them the impression that they were being micromanaged.

The expansion

Autocratic leaders adhere to the principle of structuring operations. Maintaining this structure is comparatively effortless in workplaces with borders; however, its efficacy diminishes as personnel venture beyond those boundaries. Remote employees, also known as telecommuters, perform their duties beyond the physical boundaries of the workplace. They violate numerous autocratic regulations due to their lack of adherence to a rigorous structure. They choose the location and schedule of their employment, provided they can fulfill their professional obligations.

Just a few decades ago, it was inconceivable that individuals could labor remotely from any location on Earth without encountering complications. This is no longer the case; employees can now perform their duties remotely from the convenience of their residences or any other location with internet connectivity. Regrettably, autocratic leadership diverges from the progressive perspectives espoused by alternative management styles. They impose restrictions on telecommuting due to their lack of control over the practice, which typically impedes their organizations' growth.

A sense of empathy

It is impossible to express this in any other manner than bluntly. Autocratic leaders lack comprehension of the requirements of their personnel due to their excessive emphasis on organization. Due to the absence of empathy in their inflexible management approach, their employees ultimately endure emotional hardships.

Employees are perpetually distracted from their work due to additional concerns in their personal lives. There are occasions when it is necessary to discuss such matters, and autocratic leaders may not possess the greatest listening skills. Autocrats believe that their established principles should resolve every issue, but this is not the case. For instance, an employee who has lost a family member may require time off to lament. Although the autocratic leader deems three paid days sufficient, the employee maintains that he requires additional time off. The autocrat finds this need incomprehensible because she has established regulations that prohibit it. Despite approving the additional leave, her lack of empathy prevents her from comprehending that this time is necessary and justifiable.

# I Acquired All Of My Knowledge Regarding Leadership Through Therapy.

The vast majority of leadership books that I have perused center around historical leadership models. Leaders of nations, from Moses in the Old Testament to contemporary figures such as Nelson Mandela. Almost every book on business leadership I've read centers on the CEO, be it that of Jack Welch, Steve Jobs, or another rock star CEO. Pretending leadership is frequently examined within a restricted framework. Leadership is typically associated with individuals of high social standing.

Although the reality is that the majority of us will never lead a multinational corporation or serve as the president of a powerful nation, that is not the purpose of leadership for the overwhelming majority.

As a therapist, I was responsible for guiding an individual toward significant transformation. To be a competent mentor for others, I was required to confront my neurotic tendencies as a therapist. This is the essence of transformational leadership: simultaneously transforming oneself and others.

What is the reason for transformation? The straightforward response is that nothing remains constant. Transformational leadership is crucial not because something requires modification but because circumstances are perpetually evolving. Transformational leadership is an everyday occurrence, whether in the context of business or at the individual level.

Having recently undergone an amputation, one of my most recent clients in therapy was a diabetic. As a result of his prolonged smoking following the amputation, his extremities were not receiving oxygen, and he was not recovering. He called my office to obtain assistance with quitting smoking.

Since our objective was to assist him in achieving an enduring change, my intervention with this client did not draw from my toolbox of psychological therapies but from my transformational leadership toolbox. Although we began with the understanding that change is unavoidable, we aimed to select the nature of the change he would encounter and ensure that it would be permanent. By adopting this perspective, I successfully transformed an area where opposition had hitherto existed. By utilizing transformational leadership, I was able to accompany him into a new phase of his life, one that I had also entered over a decade prior when I gave up smoking.

This form of leadership is considerably more prevalent than the focus of most leadership textbooks and training programs. As a pastor or family therapist, the likelihood is significantly greater that you will guide a small group of families through difficult times than that of becoming the pastor of a megachurch or the next Virginia Satir. Being the CEO of a big-box retailer is hardly analogous to operating a business as a small entrepreneur overseeing two to three employees, where you are significantly less likely to exercise your creative capacity. One's managerial responsibilities primarily pertain to the performance of individual employees rather than the 305,000 employees of General Electric across the globe. Personal development and the necessity for leadership skills are significantly more probable than the theoretical frameworks discussed in most leadership training manuals.

Numerous leadership books encourage readers to contemplate the future under their leadership. However, I urge you to pause momentarily while perusing this material and consider how you can effectively carry out the responsibilities of a leader in the community that you currently reside in. To attain the status of an effective transformational leader, one must initially acknowledge their transformational leadership qualities. Crucial is the inquiry: How can one attain complete self-actualization and augment their leadership prowess across various spheres—family, community, business organizations, nation, and even the globe?

Fundamentally, transformational leadership entails being in the company of others. Doing something with individuals is more important than doing something to them. I learned as a clinician that leadership is a collaborative endeavor. As a therapist, I realized the importance of being present and sitting with another person. Good therapy has been described as "bellybutton to bellybutton communication," which metaphorically characterizes the process as a reciprocal exchange that fosters the development of both the client and therapist. In essence, effective leadership fortifies the leader and those being led.

Before receiving my doctorate from Bakke Graduate University, most of my understanding of leadership had been gained through practical experience and individual counseling with clients. My understanding of leadership was strengthened through my scholarly research and dissertation. However, counseling facilitates the change process, and the therapist must assist the individual in this transformation. While this transformation may occasionally result from a voluntary choice, it is frequently unavoidable: The purpose of counseling is to alleviate the discomfort associated with the inescapable transition. This holds for community, educational, healthcare, and organizational leadership (in organizations of all sizes).

I ponder the following as I reflect on my extensive therapy career: What have I learned about leadership in therapy? It imparted to me a wealth of knowledge regarding transformational leadership:

In life, transformation is the norm. Nothing whatsoever remains the same.

The Power of Connection, Chapter 3

The immeasurable power of personal connections transcends geographical and temporal boundaries. These connections, which are formed using common experiences, sincere empathy, and mutual comprehension, have the potential to significantly influence our lives. They are a steadfast source of encouraging and powerful support amidst challenging circumstances. Personal relationships stimulate innovation and promote cooperation by facilitating the exchange of varied viewpoints and concepts, propelling development and advancement. Furthermore, they impart significance and intention to our existence, providing a feeling of inclusion and satisfaction that enhances the human condition. These familial, professional, or spiritual connections remind us of our common humanity and the extraordinary capacity for solidarity and affection that characterizes our voyage as a group.

Establishing personal connections has an exponential effect due to its capacity to generate a profound and far-reaching network of support and influence. By cultivating personal connections, individuals establish individualized relationships with others and gain access to a vast network of interconnected resources and individuals. These connections may provide access to opportunities for professional development, the exchange of knowledge, or individual progress that would have been unattainable otherwise. Moreover, the amalgamation of expertise, capabilities, and viewpoints contained within a personal network can stimulate ingenuity and resolution of issues, thereby augmenting the likelihood of inventive approaches to intricate dilemmas. Personal connections can enhance an individual's influence, prospects, and scope in both their personal and professional domains; thus, they constitute a valuable resource in the globally interconnected society of the twenty-first century.

## The Insatiable Desire for Human Connection

The human condition is intrinsically friendly, and our psychological constitution contains an insatiable desire for connection. Throughout history, humans have endeavored to establish camaraderie, communities, and bonds that have significantly influenced our evolution. Associating, empathizing, and communicating with others is intrinsic to the human condition, as the intimacy of social bonds nourishes emotional well-being. These connections provide opportunities for personal development, support, and a sense of belonging.

Early settlers in America frequently constructed their dwellings near one another for various pragmatic reasons anchored in the obstacles and circumstances they encountered. Several primary factors can be cited:

**Safety and Defence:** Constructing dwellings nearby offered protection and security against potential dangers and assaults from Native American nations, wild animals, and other external threats. It was simpler for the community to defend itself collectively in a confined settlement.

**Community Support:** The advantageous geographical position of the colonizers facilitated communication and collaboration. During periods of scarce resources, survival was frequently difficult. The proximity of neighbors facilitated the exchange of resources, tools, and expertise, thereby promoting a stronger sense of community cohesion.

Common Resources: Common resources, including water sources, grazing land for livestock, and agricultural plots, were frequently shared by the settlers. Constructing structures near one another enhanced resource utilization and promoted collaborative endeavors in agriculture and animal husbandry.

The proximity of early settlers promoted social interaction, as isolation posed a considerable obstacle for this group. This was essential for the community's emotional health and for exchanging news, ideas, and information.

Acknowledging that these justifications differed by the particular historical and geographical milieu is imperative. Settlement patterns were influenced by the distinct challenges that emanated from various regions and periods.

Companionship, solace, and a system of reciprocal assistance comprise the web of human relationships, which underpins our social and emotional welfare. In our interconnected world, exchanging ideas, opportunities, and collaboration is crucial, which propels innovation and progress. Our pursuit of meaningful connections continues to be a fundamental aspect of human nature in an ever more interconnected world; it is evidence of our collective yearning for comprehension, affection, and the common human condition.

## Healthcare Remote Work: Expanding Beyond Telemedicine

Unsurprisingly, the healthcare industry has become involved in a situation where virtually every aspect of our lives can be regulated via a digital screen. Although telemedicine is frequently used as an example of remote work in healthcare, the transition to remote operations encompasses a broader range of responsibilities, including administrative duties and patient care. Examining the inventive solutions currently being developed is warranted in response to this terrain's challenges.

The digital revolution has permeated numerous facets of our lives, including food ordering and communicating with loved ones worldwide. Healthcare, an essential component of human existence, has not been exempt from the impact of this surge. Although the discourse frequently commences with telemedicine, the true scope of remote work in healthcare encompasses considerably more, challenging conventional limits and reshaping avenues of opportunity.

One could argue that healthcare has historically been "remote." Early indicators included home visits, telephone consultations, and even mailed medical results conducted by physicians in the past. However, contemporary remote healthcare is an entirely distinct animal, propelled by innovation and technological advancements.

Routine consultations, which previously demanded an individual's human presence, have transformed. A physician based in San Francisco can now evaluate a patient's condition, review their symptoms, and prescribe medication to an individual in rural Montana via video contact. It is insufficient to simply bridge distances; efficacy must also be increased. Dermatologists may be able to see more patients via back-to-back online consultations as opposed to traditional clinic settings due to eliminating the delay associated with in-person appointments.

Nonetheless, not only physicians are making the transition. An increasing number of positions within the healthcare system are embracing remote work. Medical coding, formerly performed in an office setting, has transitioned to remote operations, with coders securely accessing patient records from their workstations. In the same way that health education and patient advocacy, both essential for managing chronic diseases such as hypertension and diabetes, have found a home on virtual platforms, educators can now reach a greater audience.

Additionally, support positions in healthcare are enduring a revolution. The IT departments maintaining healthcare infrastructure may be geographically dispersed to guarantee round-the-clock system functionality. Medical transcriptionists, once hospital fixtures, frequently transcribe doctor-patient conversations from recordings while operating remotely.

But not without its intricacies does the transition entail. The inherently intimate and profoundly personal nature of healthcare raises concerns regarding the effectiveness and morality of remote procedures. Is it possible for a psychiatrist to consult a patient effectively via video call? How do medical professionals ascertain that the patient comprehends the intricacies of a prescribed treatment or diagnosis from the other end of the screen? In the midst of this, concerns regarding the privacy and security of data loom enormous. Each online record entry and every virtual consultation constitutes a potential site of vulnerability.

Efforts are being made to improve security protocols, establish protocols for remote patient care, and provide medical professionals with the necessary training to adjust to this emerging mode of operation. Strict data access controls, end-to-end encryption, and multi-factor authentication are increasingly becoming the norm instead of the exception.

Similar to the wider transition to remote work, the transition to remote healthcare requires striking a balance between the potential for increased efficiency and accessibility and the difficulties associated with quality, security, and invaluable human connection. As the industry navigates this dynamic landscape, one thing is certain: the future of healthcare will involve reimagining where, how, and by whom care is delivered, not merely developing new medications or performing innovative procedures.

Master Effective Communication in Chapter 1.

Not only has the world in which we live, work, and lead changed significantly over the past decade, but it has been completely supplanted. This book discusses how to maintain your leadership relevance in light of the new realities of the Social Age.

The dissemination of information was profoundly transformed mid-fifteenth century. Presently, the digitization of communication and Web 2.0 are significantly reshaping the processes of information production and consumption, surpassing any previous innovation. As a result of the rapidly declining costs of communication and global social networks, we are observing a veritable revolution in how we establish and maintain new social identities based on shared interests and passions.

It is not an exaggeration to assert that, shortly, all information will be social, considering how social networks transmit data instantaneously into the social sphere. Information is being liberated, instantaneous, constant, ubiquitous, inexpensive, and liberated from temporal and geographical constraints. Integrating information into society fundamentally transforms how individuals interact with one another. Since we ceased our nomadic hunting lifestyle and embarked on the profoundly disruptive action of establishing ourselves in a single location, nothing has fundamentally altered the foundations of our existence.

This new information paradigm is causing a fundamental shift in how humans interact. This new reality, which we refer to as "the Social Age," is distinguished by the following three features:

Information socialization The emergence of interconnected global communities

The advent of the prosumer, an individual who feels entirely at ease in the Social Age

The concept of "prosumer" refers to a transition among individuals from passive consumers who purchase goods and services made for them to active contributors who collaborate with companies and each other in the design, development, and even conception of the services and products they utilize.

It is as if those of us who reached adulthood before it are immigrants into it. We must discover ways to adjust and possibly prosper in this new world. Recent immigrants to the Social Age must have been disheartened to learn that, according to a 2013 Time magazine/ABT SRBI poll, irrespective of political affiliation, believed Edward Snowden had done a good deed by leaking NSA secrets.1 In the eyes of digital natives, information serves no purpose if it is not integrated into the social domain.

Consequently, what is the Social Age that is currently emerging? The fifteen most popular social networking sites attracted 1.9 billion monthly visitors in January 2014.2 Approximately a quarter-million fresh users establish online profiles on social networks daily.3 The following data is derived from the GSM Association, an organization comprised of mobile operators and affiliated businesses:

Thirteen billion or more text messages were transmitted in 2013.

Over one thousand users register for mobile services that facilitate learning and media consumption each minute.

Sixty-four percent of mobile consumers are located in developing nations.

Rapidly gaining societal and organizational dominance, networked communities are reshaping how we operate, interact, and lead others within our organizations.

Although digital technology enables unprecedented levels of mass communication, the operation of the communication network is still primarily attributed to individuals and groups whose membership is predicated on a common interest or passion. Worldwide, one million individuals are subscribers of World of Warcraft. The number of Facebook users is comparable to the population of the world's third most populous nation. The ongoing proliferation of virtual communities is predicated on the individual interests of their constituents. We no longer understand communication as it once was; it has evolved into a conversation between you, me, and everyone who shares our passion.

A feature that distinguishes social media is that the community of information sharers determines the operation of the network. The content on Wikipedia, for instance, is managed and monitored by the user community. The confidence of the community supports eBay. Social media review platforms, including Yelp for businesses and services, Rotten Tomatoes for films, Amazon reviews for books, and Glassdoor for employers, are replacing "expert opinions" and ensuring product quality through user-generated reviews. In addition to rating and ranking the content, individuals also assess the overall quality of the evaluations. Although no " one is in charge," the community has developed into a self-regulating organism by discovering a means to monitor itself. Amid this, the subsequent paradoxes of the Social Age are coming to light:

Although we spend an ever-increasing amount of time "alone" online, our connections to one another are stronger than ever before.

Although digital technology may appear to depersonalize communication, the content and format of our exchanges are determined by our passions and interests.

# Developing High-Performing Groups: A Mastery Of Collaboration

This chapter explores the complex realm of team dynamics and development, which serve as the foundation for forming high-performing teams. Developing and directing a high-performing group is a defining characteristic of outstanding leadership. During our investigation of this field, we shall unveil the enigmatic workings of teams, decipher the intricacies involved in guiding remote and virtual teams, and furnish you with the indispensable competencies required to resolve conflicts within teams.

Building and Managing Teams: The Alchemy of Collaboration

Consider an orchestra comprising musicians, each performing a distinct instrument. By coordinating and fostering team spirit, the conductor guides individual endeavors toward completing a unified symphony. When considering leadership, it is critical to comprehend these dynamics and foster a unified team.

A Comprehension of Team Dynamics

Team dynamics comprise the processes, relationships, and interactions when individuals collaborate to achieve a common objective. These dynamics influence the communication, decision-making, and operation of a team. To delve into the foundational elements of team dynamics:

**Duties and obligations:** Each team member fulfills a distinct function and assumes obligations that contribute to the overall achievement of the group. These roles must be precisely defined to prevent confusion and redundant effort.

For example, a project team may comprise individuals with distinct responsibilities, such as a quality assurance specialist, a technical lead, and a project manager.

Transparent and open communication promotes confidence and guarantees a team's unrestricted exchange of information.
Team members must be at ease when expressing ideas, concerns, and updates during discussions and meetings.

**Leadership and the Process of Making Decisions:** Leadership can be delegated to a specific individual or a shared responsibility within a team. Clearly defined decision-making processes are essential, irrespective of whether they rely on majority vote, consensus, or another approach.

For example, a team may appoint a team leader who is tasked with the responsibility of directing deliberations and reaching ultimate resolutions.

143

**Resolution of Conflicts:** Disagreement is an inherent aspect of group dynamics. Successful teams have established processes and procedures to resolve conflicts constructively to benefit the entire group.

Teams may employ conflict resolution strategies such as mediation or facilitated discussions to resolve disputes.

Teams are committed to achieving particular aims and objectives. These objectives must be precisely defined, quantifiable, and consistent with the mission and values of the organization. For example, A quarterly revenue growth of 15% could be the objective of a sales group.

The Phases of Group Formation

Different phases of development occur as teams are formed, progress, and reach maturity. Gaining an understanding of these stages can assist leaders in effectively supporting their teams and navigating obstacles.

The following are widely acknowledged phases of team development:

The Formation During the formation phase, team members become acquainted with one another and determine the team's mission and objectives. Frequent sentiments include optimism and excitement, as well as uncertainty.

Leadership objectives and responsibilities that are crystal clear, rapport-building, and tone-setting for the team.